Teaching practice and mentoring:
The key to effective literacy, language and numeracy teacher training

Jay Derrick and Jamie Dicks

niace
the national organisation for adult learning

Published by the National Institute of Adult Continuing Education (England and Wales)
21 De Montfort Street
Leicester LE1 7GE

Company registration no. 2603322
Charity registration no. 1002775
Copyright © 2005 National Institute of Adult Continuing Education (England and Wales)

NIACE's website on the Internet is **www.niace.org.uk**

Cataloguing in Publication Data
A CIP record of this title is available from the British Library

ISBN 1 86201 237 7

Typeset by Book Production Services, London

Contents

The editors gratefully acknowledge the contribution of the following institutions, their staff and students, to the RETRO project and to this publication:

Anglia Polytechnic University
Cardinal Newman College
Dunstable College
Essex Consortia
Oaklands and Hertfordshire PDRC
Solihull College
talent London
Tower Hamlets College
University of Cambridge ESOL Examinations
University of Teesside
West Suffolk College

Introduction and acknowledgements

This booklet is aimed at practitioners, trainers, and managers of training programmes involved in literacy, language or numeracy (LLN) initial teacher education. It focuses on the issues involved in the provision of high-quality teaching practice placements and the professional mentoring required to ensure that the trainees get the most out of their teaching practice.

The training of new teachers is vital to the success of the *Skills for Life* strategy. Not only are there too few teachers at present, but the overall quality of teaching is not high enough, according to the most recent relevant OFSTED report.

Weaknesses in initial assessment and the poor quality of most Individual Learning Plans (ILPs) mean that it is difficult to assess the progress of individual learners ... There are examples of very good provision in all sectors, but most expertise is concentrated in the colleges. However, inspections of colleges show that the proportion of good provision is much lower in literacy, numeracy and ESOL than it is in any other area of learning, and there is significantly more unsatisfactory provision ... Many of the learners with the greatest need are with providers with the least qualified staff, the fewest resources and the lowest budget for staff training. This is of major concern.

From **Literacy, numeracy and English for speakers of other languages: a survey of current practice in Post-16 and Adult provision**, OFSTED, September 2003

Teaching practice is one of the most important elements of initial teacher training, but in the Post-16 sector it has often played a secondary or even minor role. The publication of *Success for All*, the new LLUK (Lifelong Learning UK, formerly FENTO) standards, and the national *Skills for Life* strategy, have all given a new prominence to teaching practice as part of training. Most significantly, last year the DfES Standards Unit published *Equipping our Teachers for the Future*, which calls for 'a step change in the quality of teacher training', outlines a major reform programme accompanied by substantial new funding, and highlights the role of teaching practice and the need for professional mentoring of teachers in the workplace.

> *Subject-specific skills must be acquired in the teachers' workplace and from vocational or academic experience. Mentoring, either by line managers, subject experts or experienced teachers in related curriculum areas, is essential....*
>
> *The vast majority of teachers in the learning and skills sector are trained in-service and model their future practice by observing colleagues and mentors who teach the same subject or vocational area. Without good role models of teaching and comprehensive support, their development is severely inhibited.*
>
> **From *Equipping our Teachers for the Future*, DfES, 2004**

In this booklet we aim to support the process of developing a new and in-depth look at all aspects of teaching practice, in particular by disseminating a range of different organisational approaches being taken by different programmes across the country. We hope that this will encourage managers of training programmes to be more imaginative in designing teaching practice opportunities for their trainees, remembering that this is a pedagogical issue as well as an organisational one. We also hope to remind such managers of the key role that can be played in teaching practice by mentors – the experienced teachers who lead the placement groups in which the trainees get their teaching practice. The importance of their role is highlighted in last year's OFSTED survey of initial teacher-training programmes in further education:

> *The current system of FE teacher training does not provide a satisfactory foundation of professional development for FE teachers at the start of their careers....*
>
> *Few trainees receive effective mentoring in the workplace, and their progress is inhibited by insufficient observation and feedback on their teaching....*
>
> *Too little attention is given to trainees' action planning and setting realistic targets for improvement against the LLUK standards....*
>
> *Observation of trainees' teaching does not have a high enough profile in their assessment, and procedures are insufficient to guarantee that someone awarded a teaching qualification is competent in the classroom or workshop ... HEIs and national awarding bodies should give substantially more attention to developing trainees' expertise in teaching their subject, and ensure that the trainees' practical teaching is made more central to their training and assessment*
>
> **From *The initial training of further education teachers, a survey*, OFSTED, 2003**

In practice, most teacher educators report difficulties in providing high-quality supported teaching practice opportunities for their trainees. In part, this is a consequence of the overall shortage of LLN teachers, but also it reflects the relatively low level of professional development of many LLN teachers working at present, and this in turn may account for some of the weaknesses reported by OFSTED. Another factor is that the experienced teachers who lead the teaching practice sessions and support the trainees informally as mentors are hardly ever offered any recognition or recompense for the work involved, in the form of training, career development, extra payment, or remission from teaching. A further issue is that trainees are rarely offered teaching practice in more than one setting. A fully-qualified LLN teacher will usually have received all their teaching practice within a college, yet they are formally qualified to teach in prisons, workplaces, community settings, and Learndirect centres as well.

So, the situation is that there are often not enough placements for teaching practice, and in most cases not enough different kinds of teaching practice placement on offer to trainees. As the OFSTED survey emphasises, this is not just a logistical problem, but an issue of quality, as well-supported teaching practice is a central element of a successful training course.

This guide is intended to help improve this situation. It focuses mainly on the initial training of LLN teachers, but is relevant to most teacher education in Post-16. It is based on practical teacher training development and support projects from all over the country that have grappled with the many challenges training-course providers face in finding practice placements for their trainees, and in finding high-quality mentors to support them. It aims to identify common difficulties in providing teaching-practice opportunities and provide ideas for addressing them.

We argue for a strategic partnership approach to planning the teaching-practice elements of training programmes, and suggest ways that this can be arranged. We believe there is a strong case for improved core funding for initial teacher education, on the grounds that the present system does not account for the costs of providing high-quality teaching practice and professional mentor support.

We start by discussing what is meant by teaching practice and mentoring, and by defining our terms. We move on to clarify the importance and location of initial teacher training, teaching practice and mentoring within the national *Skills for Life* strategy. In chapter 3 we discuss the teacher training team and make the case for the full inclusion of teaching practice mentors. This has the implication that teams are likely to straddle a number of different partnership organisations. Chapter 4 outlines five different models for the organisation of teaching practice and argues that trainees should have experience of a range of these models. Chapter 5 deals with observations of teaching practice, and giving feedback; chapter 6 looks at the specific training needs of teaching practice mentors; and chapter 7 discusses developing and sustaining new placements for teaching practice. We conclude with chapter on approaches to quality assurance of teaching practice and mentoring. The booklet finishes with a reference section, which includes a list of useful organisations and their websites, a list of useful references and a glossary.

We are well aware that there is much expertise and experience, and many relevant publications, that we have not made reference to: in a booklet of this size we can only hope to raise issues and stimulate discussion and debate.

The main sources of the ideas and models in this booklet are **talent London,** funded by the London Development Agency, which supports partnership working in LLN teacher training and professional development across the London region; and RETRO (Recruitment and Training Opportunities for new literacy, language and numeracy teachers), a DfES/SfLSU-funded project managed by NIACE which developed models for regional infrastructures for initial teacher training, and tested in three regions: the North East, Birmingham and the West Midlands, and the Eastern Region. Many staff in these projects have contributed time and materials referred to in the booklet, and in particular we would like to thank Sally Bird, Suzanne Goodwin, Kath Dodd, Mark Barnsley, Naomi Horrocks, and Jo-Ann Delaney.

Chapter 1
What is meant by teaching practice and mentoring? Why is it important?

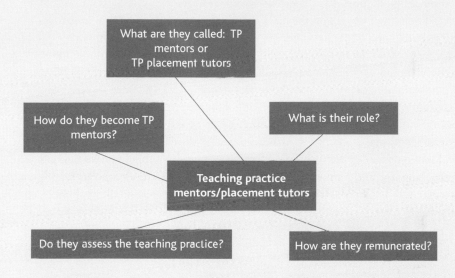

In this chapter we look at the role of teaching practice and the teaching practice mentor within teacher training, and argue for increased formalisation and recognition of this role.

Anybody wishing to work as a teacher or trainer in the post-16 sector now needs to be qualified, or aiming to qualify, against demanding standards set by FENTO (now LLUK: see glossary). The standards make clear what skills and knowledge teachers must demonstrate they have, depending on the level at which they need to qualify: level 3 or level 4 within the National Qualifications Framework (NQF). Teacher training programmes are offered by approved organisations, and mostly take place in further education colleges (FE) or in higher education institutions (HEIs). A key requirement of all approved teacher training qualifications at any of these levels is that trainees must have teaching practice as part of their training. **Teaching practice involves trainees working in real classes with real learners alongside fully-qualified professional teachers.** This element of the education of teachers is vital, because teaching is a matter of practice as well as of knowledge or theory. It is during their teaching practice that trainee teachers put their training to the test and reflect on it, watch experienced teachers at work, and gain experience of the wide range of learning needs and attitudes to learning displayed by students. Teaching practice is also formally observed as an element of the assessment of the trainee. Setting up placements in which the trainees can get their teaching practice, supporting them in their placement, and incorporating their reflections on it as part of the overall training programme, is an essential part of any teacher trainer's job.

If the trainee is placed for their teaching practice directly into a class, the experienced teacher responsible is called the teaching practice mentor (TP mentor, or TPM). Teachers who agree to take on this role play an important part in the training process, as important in many ways as the teacher trainer's role. As well as being responsible for the learning of their students, they help trainees get experience in lesson planning and teaching, and support them in their first experiences of working with learners. One of their most important tasks as TP mentors is to act as a role model for trainees, demonstrating good practice in planning, teaching and assessing learners. They also give feedback on the activities led by the trainees, essential for the trainees to develop reflective practice and a range of teaching and assessment strategies.

The origins of the word 'mentor' go back to the Greek epic poem The Odyssey. According to the myth, when Odysseus went away to fight, he left his son Telemachus in the care of a friend named Mentor. Mentor was also a tutor to Telemachus. The name 'mentor' has, therefore become proverbial for a wise and faithful advisor. A close reading of the myth reveals the relationship between Telemachus and Mentor to have been of mutual benefit, with some versions of the myth even reporting that Telemachus saved Mentor's life.

Association of Colleges in the Eastern Region, Teacher Training Unit, Mentoring Handbook
http://www.acer.ac.uk/newtrainingthetrainers/training_material.html

---

Some people take 'mentor' to mean 'peer', a person in the same boat, who gives you feedback and suggestions. For others, it means a 'critical friend' – someone who guides you in a more structured way. Some understand it to mean the person who assesses your teaching in a formal way by giving you written formative/developmental feedback or even summative feedback. The word mentor is also sometimes given a more specific meaning in which it is applied to an experienced colleague supporting a new recruit in the workplace, rather than on a pre-service training course.

This booklet uses *teaching practice placement tutor* (**TPPT**) and *TP mentor* **interchangeably**. We are happy for 'TP mentor' to be used in the context of initial teacher training, because, in any case, many of the teachers gaining their first qualifications at Level 4 are already experienced and employed teachers. In particular, we want to distinguish clearly between the roles of TP mentors and trainers, and this distinction will be elaborated in the following chapters. In some situations, mentors receive peer support, either as part of formal systems or informally. We think that trainees will benefit most from having all three different kinds of support in their training, and from these being clearly separated where possible. Nevertheless we also argue that TP mentors should be seen as full members of the training team, with all the organisational and political implications that follow from this, in order to demonstrate that teaching practice is at the heart of effective teacher education programmes.

> **Recommendations for mentors:**
>
> • *Mentors should have job descriptions that clarify their role.*
> • *Mentoring should be part of the management's commitment to improving quality and raising standards of teaching and learning.*
> • *Mentors should be formally trained.*
> • *Mentors should either be paid for mentoring, or given time to carry out the job.*
> • *Mentoring should be used to increase the sharing of good practice.*
>
> **From *Mentoring Towards Excellence, LSC, AoC and FENTO*, 2001**

Chapter 2
Initial teacher training and
Skills for Life

In this chapter, we outline the Skills for Life strategy and discuss the role of teacher training within it. We clarify the new regulations governing the qualifications demanded of professionals teaching and supporting learning in literacy, language and numeracy, and then discuss the challenges presented to teacher training by Skills for Life.

Skills for Life is the national strategy for improving adult literacy, language and numeracy in England and Wales. It is co-ordinated by the *Skills for Life* Strategy Unit (SfLSU, formerly ABSSU) which is based in the Department for Education and Skills (DfES). The unit has produced national standards for LLN, curriculum documents, learning and assessment materials and national tests for literacy and numeracy. It commissions development projects and has set up the National Research and Development Centre for adult literacy and numeracy (NRDC). It has also initiated the implementation of national standards and new qualifications for the training of *Skills for Life* teachers.

The FENTO standards for teacher training qualifications in further education are published by LLUK and apply to both generic teacher training, and subject specialisms. People wanting to train as literacy, language or numeracy teachers need to gain both generic teacher training qualifications and subject specialist qualifications in order to be fully qualified. Within *Skills for Life*, the specialist subjects are, at present, Literacy, English for Speakers of Other Languages (ESOL), Numeracy and ICT. Each of these subjects has separate specialist training standards and programmes. All of these standards are available on the web at the LLUK website. LLUK also endorses programmes which satisfy these standards, submitted for approval by a wide range of teacher training providers throughout the country, and publishes a list of these at its website. Some providers utilise programmes already approved rather than developing new ones.

The qualifications available are part of the national qualifications framework (see glossary). Generic teacher training qualifications are set at level 4 (equivalent to degree level), and subject specialist qualifications at levels 3 and 4. A fully-qualified adult numeracy teacher needs generic and subject specialist qualifications at level 4. Level 3 qualifications are for learning support workers, and for teachers qualified in other subjects, vocational or otherwise, who offer support to learners to develop LLN. Level 2 qualifications are intended for volunteers working alongside fully-qualified teachers in LLN classes, and for a wide range of para-professional staff such as employment advisors or community health workers, whose work can be enhanced by a greater awareness of LLN issues in relation to their particular client group. Programmes that satisfy these criteria can be offered in a variety of formats: the generic and specialist qualifications can be integrated or separate, delivered in three stages or all together in one programme.

Training programmes are delivered by approved training providers. Level 3 programmes, and stages 1 and 2 of initial teacher training courses at level 4 can be provided by FE colleges. Stage 3 of the Level 4 qualifications is usually, but not always, delivered through an HEI. Whichever organisation is the formal provider of any particular course, it is likely that more than one organisation is collaborating. For example, an HE-based course may be using a college, community centre and/or workplace for the teaching practice placement.

An increasing trend is for **regional partnerships** to be established, supporting teacher training provision across a region. Bringing together different providers and stakeholders is helpful at a practical level, for example in finding placements for teaching practice. But such partnerships can also co-ordinate responses to the national *Skills for Life* strategy, strategic planning, needs analysis, and bids for funding. A strategic approach can make the best of short-term project funding to build and sustain provider partnerships and the quality of programmes over longer time periods.

The *Skills for Life* agenda presents two major challenges for teacher training. The first is **capacity planning**: the national *Skills for Life* targets imply significant expansion in the volume of provision, and this in turn implies the need for many more teachers. This is all the more urgent because of the age profile of the existing workforce. The experience of RETRO and **talent London** is that regional-level strategic planning is the best way to address this challenge.

The second major challenge is the **weaknesses in quality** identified in initial teacher training programmes and in the teaching of Literacy, Numeracy and ESOL by OFSTED. Inspection grades in the LLN programme areas continue to be lower than for other programme areas. Too many teaching sessions are inadequately planned, unfocused on learners' needs, and ineffective at helping learners to progress. Again, experience suggests that regional partnerships can be effective mechanisms for improving quality, by building and sustaining communities of practice among teachers and trainers, whichever sector they are working in.

Chapter 3
The initial teacher training team

This chapter discusses the implications for team working in the context of partnership and collaboration between staff in different organisations in the delivery of effective teacher training programmes. It argues for the importance of role clarification and the need to improve the status of teaching practice mentors, as in teacher training for the schools sector.

Training programmes for teachers of adult literacy, language and numeracy are formally delivered by a single host institution, such as a college or a university. But, in fact, few courses are wholly delivered within one institution. A university-based programme, for example, usually needs to have arrangements in place with other organisations which provide the teaching practice placements for the trainee teachers. The training programme is sometimes delivered as a partnership between an HEI and a college, with staff from both organisations working together as a team. This kind of arrangement bridges the gap between the academic world and the world of practitioners, the team-working acting as important and valuable professional development for both groups of staff.

Effective partnerships linking colleges, higher education institutions and other providers are also critical to effective initial teacher training. It is through continuous engagement in partnerships that both teacher trainers and trainee teachers are brought into contact with good practice from other organisations and are able to gain wider knowledge of the learning and skills sector.

From *Equipping our Teachers for the Future*, DfES, 2004

In principle, it is desirable for teacher training programmes to be designed as practical partnerships, both for staff development purposes and to ensure that practical and logistical issues are addressed consistently. The organisation and support for teaching-practice placements, if not carefully planned, quality-assured and carried out, can easily be an unrewarding experience for trainees, and, indeed, this was a common finding of the OFSTED survey.

The key to avoiding potential problems, all too likely in a primarily bureaucratic arrangement between two large organisations, is to see all the staff who contribute to the learning of the trainees as members of the course team, whichever organisation they formally work for. Thus a combined PGCE and

Level 4 literacy specialist course team, based in different collaborating organisations, might be made up of:

• course tutor;
• other PGCE trainers;
• literacy specialist trainers;
• teacher educators;
• teaching practice mentors;
• manager of the mentors (if many in the same institution);
• learning support tutors;
• course administrator.

Involving all these people (some of whom may play more than one role) will reduce the likelihood of organisational problems as well as helping to develop all the team members. Well-organised team-working may have a cost attached, for example in terms of meeting time, but will almost always produce benefits in terms of a smoother running programme, fewer problems caused by unforeseen circumstances, a better experience for the trainees, and higher retention. Furthermore, there will be important organisational benefits from the raised status of the teaching-practice mentors which will contribute to the sharing of good practice among their colleagues and encourage other experienced teachers to consider becoming mentors and/or trainers. Different programmes may set up different arrangements in terms of who does what, but it is important that each person's role is clear and distinct, so that trainees can get the support they need from the right member of the team.

We now look in more detail at the role of the TP mentor.

The role of TP mentors

It is essential for the team to agree on the roles, responsibilities and rights of TP mentors. All parties involved – the TP mentors, the trainee, the teacher-trainer and the placement organisation – must share the same definition of the role. Here is an example (recall that we are using 'TP mentor' and 'teaching practice placement tutor' interchangeably):

Roles and responsibilities of teaching practice placement tutors

- *To inform trainees about learners' basic skills learning needs, e.g. pace of teaching, learning goals, additional learning needs.*
- *To negotiate realistic learner/trainee contact hours.*
- *To liaise with and give feedback to lead body/course co-ordinator.*
- *To create a phased approach for teaching practice, i.e. starting with observing the group, leading to whole-group teaching.*
- *To model teaching methodology to the trainee.*
- *To know the TP [teaching practice] requirements of the course in terms of placement hours and observation schedule.*
- *To have an overview of the teacher training course assignment/coursework requirements.*
- *To support the trainee teacher with scheme of work writing.*
- *To support the trainee teacher with lesson planning.*
- *To offer constructive feedback and comments on teaching, orally and informally.*
- *To keep an overview of the syllabus and accreditation goals for the students.*
- *To maintain responsibility for the class during the lessons.*
- *To liaise with the trainee teachers' course tutors.*
- *To invite the trainee teacher to course team meetings as an observer (when appropriate).*
- *To provide the trainee with information about the course, the learners and the organisation (while maintaining confidentiality).*
- *Do a formal observation if required (e.g. City & Guilds Level 4 Stages 1 and 2).*

talent London, January 2004

Formal assessment of teaching practice

The last point on the list above is the most contentious – whether or not TP mentors should formally observe and assess trainees. A formal observation is one which is conducted as summative assessment against a set of criteria which come from the awarding body for the particular course. We recommend that TP mentors only give informal informative feedback to trainees as a 'critical friend', particularly in the early stages of training. However high the level of teaching expertise of the teaching practice mentors, they are less likely than the teacher-trainer to have to have received training or to be paid to give formal, summative assessment to trainee teachers. To thrust this responsibility onto them in addition to their other responsibilities as mentors is neither in their best interests nor those of the trainee teachers. The key contributions of the mentor are role-modelling, demonstration of good practice, informal support and the ongoing formative assessment of the trainee – this vital, close and more informal relationship is likely to be inhibited or even compromised if they also play a formal assessment role. However, as many institutions are now designing accredited TP mentor courses at undergraduate or graduate level which incorporate training in giving formal assessment to trainees, we will look at a range of models later in this guide. We also believe that visits to the teaching practice sessions by the HEI-based trainers are an important part of ensuring the links between the formal tuition and the teaching practice elements of the programme are strong, and that formal observations and assessment provide a natural mechanism for strengthening these links.

Clear definition of roles is one of the foundations of professional competence and status, and is the reason why formalising the work of TP mentors is so important for improving quality and consistency in teacher training. Too often, as the OFSTED report suggests, support for teaching practice has not been treated as a key role within teacher training programmes, and, as a result, has taken place haphazardly. One implication of improving this situation is that the work of TP mentors will need to be subjected to quality standards and specific professional training, and will consequently need to be recognised in terms of staff workload, remuneration, and career development. In particular, it is important to implement a selection process for TP mentors. Some RETRO partnerships have produced guidelines for this based on agreed personal qualities and skills, and the Eastern region has also developed a self-assessment exercise for teachers considering becoming mentors.

Mentoring, capacity-building, and career development

To sustain quality improvement and achievement in LLN teacher training, mentoring trainees needs to become a regular part of the work of all experienced teachers of adult LLN. Giving the work formal status in terms of workload, career development, and increased remuneration, as is the norm in teacher training for the schools sector, will increase the supply, diversity and quality of teaching practice placements, raise the confidence and professionalism of LLN teachers, and support more new entrants to the teaching profession. At present very many mentors, perhaps the majority, take on the role out of professional commitment, with little expectation of professional training or support, career development, increased pay, or even any remission of their teaching load. For the quality of teacher training to improve, and to sustain that improvement, this has to change. This is a key challenge for funding agencies and for the employers of LLN teachers.

Chapter 4
Models and settings for teaching practice:
The 'scaffolded approach'

In this chapter we look at the organisation of teaching practice within teacher education. We outline a variety of different organisational models, discuss each model in terms of its pedagogical role, and argue that trainees should experience different models of teaching practice as part of their programme.

The element of teaching practice in a teacher training course has an enormous effect on the trainee. A good placement with the right level of support often enables the trainee to blossom as a teacher. A problematic placement can severely restrict the trainee's development, hampering her/him from putting theory into practice or taking risks. Few dispute the need to improve the quality of TP placements: the question is, how to achieve it.

The first aspect of TP placements to address is the model of placements. The traditional strategy for teaching practice is to place trainees individually in a setting. At the moment, most trainees, whether on generic teacher training courses or subject-specific courses, are dispersed, and placed on their own in colleges or community classes, attached to a teacher who becomes their placement tutor/mentor.

Talent London proposes a more staged approach. It is as follows: rather than the teacher training team opting for a system of individual placements from the outset, the team can provide a range of TP practice situations. This entails using paired or group placements at the beginning of teacher training, then phasing in individual placements. Adopting this approach allows for varying levels of support for trainees at different stages of their teacher training. **Talent London** have called this the 'scaffolded approach' to teaching practice. This chapter will explore this scheme further.

In education, the concept of scaffolding (Bruner, 1975) is based on the work of Vygotsky. It is taken to mean 'a process in which students are given support until they can apply new skills and strategies independently' (Rosenshine &

Meister, 1992). **Talent London** have extended the use of the term 'scaffolding' to refer to a method of organising teaching practice. A 'scaffolded approach' to teaching practice means that trainees progress from a situation where they share a placement with other trainees to a TP teaching practice situation where they are more independent.

In the same way that language/literacy learners are given example texts and guided/'scaffolded' writing activities before free writing, trainee teachers should be entitled to a broad range of support at the beginning of their teaching practice experience.

> *When students are learning new or difficult tasks, they are given more assistance. As they begin to demonstrate task mastery, the assistance or support is decreased gradually in order to shift the responsibility for learning from the teacher to the students. Thus, as the students assume more responsibility for their learning, the teacher provides less support.*

Larkin, 2001

There are a number of drawbacks to the current model of using individual placements at the outset of ITT. If trainees are placed immediately in classes with a TP mentor, too much then depends on the quality of support provided by that person/TP mentor. Trainees in individual placements have little peer support. They can compare notes with other trainees, but those trainees do not share experience of the same group of learners. Rather, they all speak from the perspective of their own group of learners, who are not known to the other trainees. The only other person they see teaching 'their' learners is a highly experienced and qualified teacher, who may make teaching look deceptively easy. In fact, in individual placements, trainees seldom see one another teach at all, so they can't learn from one another's mistakes and successes. Trainees may receive fewer support visits from their trainers once they are attached to a TP mentor.

The current system, therefore, often relies heavily on support from a TP mentor while at the same time leaving the quality of this support somewhat to chance, in that no training is required of mentors. These TP mentors can be excellent role models and are often extremely supportive to teachers in initial training. However, this is not always the case. The TP mentors usually have high levels of responsibility with little or no training or remuneration. In the post-16 context, TP mentors are seldom given pay, remission or training.

Talent London advocates a 'scaffolded approach', whereby a range of different models are used on all teacher training courses. It involves phasing in these individual/independent placements, starting trainees off in a group or paired TP placement. Trainees are then gradually weaned off the more supportive environment of group or paired placements on to individual placements later in their training. The issue of training TP mentors will be explored in chapter 6.

The 'scaffolded approach' to teaching practice

There are at least five ways to organise teaching practice, from using training groups to using a trainee's own paid employment. A description of each model of TP placement follows, together with a summary of the strengths and weaknesses of each type. Each of the placement models below is already being used nationally. What is new is the proposal that all trainees should experience a range of placement models. There is a diagrammatic version of these models on the facing page.

Model One: Training groups

In the first model, a team sets up practice teaching classes then puts trainees into the classes in groups as the first part of trainees' teaching practice. This type of arrangement is normally found in initial training courses such as the Cambridge ESOL CELTA, the Trinity Certificate Level 4 Stage 2 or Literacy teacher training, but it could equally well be the first phase of a full certificate/ PGCE course. In a training course for twelve trainees, two groups of practice learners can be arranged for a term. Typically this is in a local college, using either existing classes or volunteer learners. Two teacher trainers have overall responsibility for the learners as well as for the trainee teachers who are divided into two TP groups. There are no TP placement tutors or mentors. The teacher trainers liaise with the college teacher who normally takes the class. Together they devise the scheme of work, linked to the literacy, numeracy or ESOL curriculum. Each individual teaching session is then co-planned with the teacher trainer and the trainees. The trainees (A–F on the grid, pp 24–5) subsequently teach a portion of the planned lesson, while their peers and trainer watch supportively at the back of the classroom. Trainees build up gradually to teaching a full hour as illustrated in the sample teaching practice grid on pp, 24–5 for a group of six trainees with one trainer. The other six trainees would have a similar schedule with the other trainer.

The 'scaffolded approach' to teaching practice

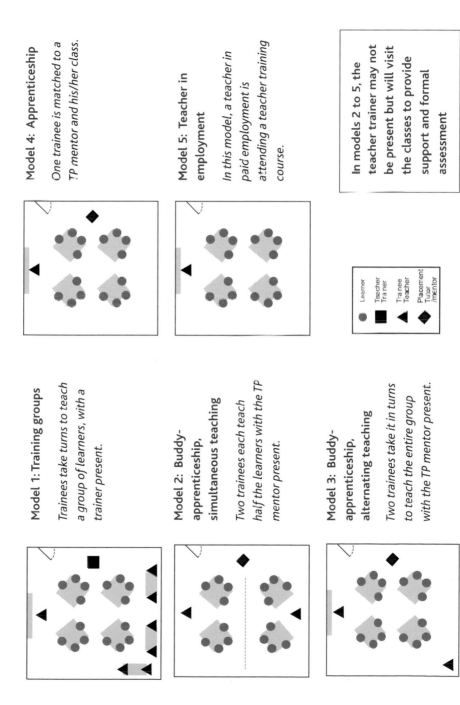

Model 1: Training groups

Trainees take turns to teach a group of learners, with a trainer present.

Model 2: Buddy-apprenticeship, simultaneous teaching

Two trainees each teach half the learners with the TP mentor present.

Model 3: Buddy-apprenticeship, alternating teaching

Two trainees take it in turns to teach the entire group with the TP mentor present.

Model 4: Apprenticeship

One trainee is matched to a TP mentor and his/her class.

Model 5: Teacher in employment

In this model, a teacher in paid employment is attending a teacher training course.

In models 2 to 5, the teacher trainer may not be present but will visit the classes to provide support and formal assessment

Learner
Teacher Trainer
Trainee Teacher
Placement Tutor /mentor

Cambridge ESOL CELTA teaching practice grid for six traineees

		A	B	C	D	E	F
1	25 Sept.	All input session					
2	2 Oct.	All input session					
3	9 Oct.	Demonstration lesson + meeting the learners					
4	16 Oct.	15 minutes	15 minutes	15 minutes	15 minutes	15 minutes	15 minutes
	Half Term						
5	30 Oct.	30 minutes	30 minutes	30 minutes			
6	6 Nov.				30 minutes	30 minutes	30 minutes
7	13 Nov.	30 minutes	30 minutes	30 minutes			
8	20 Nov.				30 minutes	30 minutes	30 minutes
9	27 Nov.	45 minutes	45 minutes				
10	4 Dec.			45 minutes	45 minutes		
11	11 Dec.					45 minutes	45 minutes
12	18 Dec.	All input					
	Christmas Holidays						
13	8 Jan.	45 minutes	45 minutes				
14	15 Jan.			45 minutes	45 minutes		
15	22 Jan.					45 minutes	45 minutes
16	29 Jan.	Demonstration lesson + meeting the new learners					
17	5 Feb.	30 minutes	30 minutes	30 minutes			
18	12 Feb				30 minutes	30 minutes	30 minutes

		A	B	C	D	E	F
19	19 Feb.	30 minutes	30 minutes	30 minutes			
	Half Term						
20	5 Mar.		30 minutes	30 minutes	30 minutes		
21	12 Mar.	45 minutes	45 minutes				
22	19 Mar.			45 minutes	45 minutes		
23	26 Mar.					45 minutes	45 minutes
24	2 Apr.	60 minutes			30 minutes		
25	9 Apr.		60 minutes		30 minutes		
	Easter Holidays						
26	30 Apr.			60 minutes			30 minutes
27	7 May.	30 minutes			60 minutes		
28	14 May.		30 minutes		60 minutes		
29	21 May.			30 minutes			60 minutes
	(Totals)	360 minutes	360 minutes	360 minutes	360 minutes	360 minutes	360 minutes
	Half Term						

As can be seen from the grid, sometimes the teacher trainer takes the class for a demonstration session. After the sessions, the trainees and the trainers have a feedback session together, discussing what went well for the learners and why. Although the grid accounts for only six hours teaching practice per trainee, all teaching is assessed by the trainers, which allows for a developmental approach at the outset of the trainee's experience.

Strengths of training groups for teaching practice

- Everyone makes suggestions on the basis of a shared experience with a known group of learners.
- Trainees learn from watching each other and develop a support network to carry them into the next phase of their TP. They develop ways of working collaboratively and offering mutual support.
- Trainees benefit from co-planning the teaching practice with their peers and their teacher trainers.
- They get a lot of feedback from the teacher trainer and their peers. They are also assessed and receive written feedback on each TP with praise and clear targets for development.
- Trainees learn from watching the teacher trainer .
- Teacher trainers can set practice teaching tasks to ensure trainees try out a range of methods and cover a range of subject knowledge.
- It is an intensive model in which trainees learn a lot very fast.
- If the two groups of trainees swap over to the other group of learners, trainees can practise working at two different levels or in two different contexts.
- The model saves enormously on travel time for trainers.

Challenges of training groups for teaching practice

• Set-up and organisation both need a lot of work.
• The relationship between teacher trainer, class tutor and institution needs to be sound.
• The teaching needs to be set up sensitively and carefully to avoid anxiety among trainees.
• Trainees need to be trained in how to give peer feedback.

LLN Tutor Trainers at the Community College Hackney and Tower Hamlets College have used the training-in-groups model of teaching practice on the Literacy specialist 7407 Stage 2 courses. The model involves groups of six trainees working with one group of learners, jointly planning and evaluating one another's sessions. One or two individual trainees teach the group each week, building up from 45-minute slots to a full 90 minutes. Although initially daunted, trainees felt that the support and constructive comments provided by both trainers and peers was extremely valuable, and equipped them well for teaching their own classes. Senior lecturers at The Community College Hackney were so impressed with the quality of trainees that they wrote to the trainers saying: 'It is clear that the developmental guidance and support, along with opportunities for reflection that this model of teaching practice offers, is producing tutors who are far better equipped to deal with the demands of classroom teaching than tutors coming off other courses such as PGCEs.' Tower Hamlets College are now using this TP model on their 7407 Stage 1 literacy or ESOL courses.

Model Two: Buddy-apprenticeship with simultaneous teaching

This model is typically used in the early training of literacy or ESOL teachers. For twelve trainees, six classes of learners and two teacher trainers are needed. Each trainer takes responsibility for three classes with the help of a teaching practice placement tutor for each class. Two trainees work in a classroom together, each trainee taking half the learners. In some colleges with large classes, this model has been extended to enable four or five trainees to teach simultaneously with the TP mentor in overall charge of the group under the supervision of the teacher trainers. The TP placement tutor supports the trainees in their planning and helps with feedback. For example, over a period of six three-hour sessions, each trainee teaches the entire 18 hours. They simply teach a smaller group. There is one visit from the teacher trainer, who assesses each of the trainees. The teacher trainers also provide training for the teaching practice placement tutors.

At the Community College Hackney on the City & Guilds 7407 Stage 1 ESOL Teacher Training, the team adopted this model:

The C & G 7407 Stage 1 ESOL course ran over 18 weeks, 14 of which included TP. The TP took place in the mornings. We had 12 trainees who were divided into two groups of six. We used two mainstream ESOL classes where the trainees taught the learners in small groups of three or four. This meant we also had the expertise of the class tutors, who helped in observation and feedback (and fulfilled the course requirement of being observed by a subject specialist). The course tutors divided the learners into 'ability' groups of weaker and stronger students and the trainers allocated trainees to a particular group. The classroom was set up for group work and the small group teaching happened simultaneously.

The trainees started teaching from week 4 of the course when they carried out an initial assessment of their particular group of students, which included assessing their speaking, listening, reading and writing skills. This gave them an overview of their learners' needs and a stepping stone to preparing materials.

The teaching session lasted two hours. As two hours seemed a very long and intense time to be doing small group teaching, we started with the trainers running whole class warmers. This helped to integrate trainees and learners as a whole, and gave the trainees an opportunity to observe more ESOL teaching and to consider activities and to understand how language can be broken down for (teaching and) learning. Towards the end of the course all trainees had the opportunity to do some whole class teaching.

Each teaching session was followed by feedback and then a TP prep session. The feedback sessions offered the opportunity to share the teaching experience and problems (and solutions that may have arisen).

In TP prep we supplied the trainees with material, which they would then need to adapt for their particular group of learners. The trainees could then work with others who had similar ability learners and discuss and plan how to adapt the materials and how to integrate what had been learnt from input sessions.

TP was a very successful experience for all. The trainees felt it less daunting to teach small groups than to begin by teaching a whole class of learners. They gradually learnt to understand the needs of their particular students, their strengths, weaknesses and built up strong positive relationships. As their confidence grew, so they became ready to stand in front of the whole class and try out an activity.

The learners enjoyed the individualised attention they received and felt their needs were being met in a way that doesn't happen in whole class teaching. Attendance was always high, and they responded well to the whole class warmers and there was always a buzzing feeling in the classroom. We ended the teaching with a class party, and the learners were sad to see the trainees go.

As the trainees on our Stage 1 have little or no previous teaching experience, this was a very positive initiation into ESOL teaching and learners, and gave them a more intimate understanding of the teaching and learning process as well as of the learners.

Report from Barbara Labjieko.

Strengths of the buddy-apprenticeship with simultaneous teaching

- Learners can be grouped in different ways to suit their needs, e.g. they can be taught at different levels, or the trainees can work on different skills, then swap over the learners.
- Very time efficient – travel for trainers and trainees is kept to a minimum.
- Trainees share the planning and support each other.
- Formal assessment is carried out by the teacher trainer, while the TPM gives developmental suggestions.
- TP mentors fulfil the role of 'critical friend' rather than assessor. They gradually take more responsibility in the later phases of the scaffolded approach.
- The involvement of a TP mentor in the programme is often the first step towards becoming trained and qualified as a teacher trainer.

Challenges of the buddy-apprenticeship with simultaneous teaching

- Trainees cannot observe each other.
- Careful organisation needed and liaison through team meetings with the TP mentor.
- TP mentors need effective training in their role.
- Noise level could be high.

Model Three: Buddy-apprenticeship alternating teaching

For this model, the same number of classes, teacher trainers and TP mentors are needed: six classes of learners, two teacher trainers and six teaching practice placement tutors – the teachers of the six classes. Trainees work in the classroom together, taking half the lesson each, e.g. 90 minutes each in a three-hour class. Over a period of 12 three-hour sessions, each trainee teaches for 18 hours. There is one visit from the teacher trainer who assesses each of the trainees.

Strengths of the buddy-apprenticeship alternating teaching model

• All the strengths of the simultaneous teaching pertain apart from the first point.
• Trainees benefit from watching each other teach a known group.

Challenges of the buddy-apprenticeship alternating teaching model

• Trainees need sound training in how to give peer feedback.
• As above in that placement tutors need effective training for their role and that the organisation of the placement has to be effective.

Model Four: Apprenticeship

This is normally the starting place for our trainees in Post-16 teaching. For twelve trainees, twelve classes of learners and twelve TP mentors are needed. This is also a well-established model for training primary and secondary school teachers – a trainee is attached to one class and has a placement tutor. At primary and secondary level, the placement tutors are paid and trained for their roles.

Strengths of the Apprenticeship model

• Trainee has support from the TP mentor.

Challenges of the Apprenticeship model

• Matching the TP mentor and trainee require substantial forethought.
• Brings high level of responsibility for placement mentor, therefore assumes that there is support and/or training available for them.
• Can be challenging for trainees to be compared to a highly qualified and experienced teacher.
• Teacher trainer has little control of the teaching practice.

> *A great deal of thought must go into matching trainees to their TP placement tutors. If it goes well, both sides respect and help each other. But good matches don't just happen, they require planning. For example, independent trainees, who may have taught before or have a lot of confidence and skills, can cope with a very busy TP mentor/tutor. Others trainees with lower confidence may need extra support so it is best to place them in the classrooms of the trainers on the course. It is important to get to know the trainees before arranging placements so you can take their personalities and interests into account.*
>
> **Teacher Training for Skills for Life at Westminster Kingsway College**

Model Five: Teacher in employment

Over the last 20 years, due to the enormous demand for LLN teachers and the shortage of training for them, some tutors have been appointed with little or no formal teacher training. In an ideal situation, these tutors will have 'learned on the job' and had access to effective continuing professional development. One of the changes as a result of the *Skills for Life* programme is that these teachers are now required to seek training opportunities for themselves in order to become fully qualified in the new framework. Model 5 is often found at Level 4 Stage 3 training, with the 'trainee' already in paid employment while training to become fully qualified.

Strengths of teacher-in-training-and-paid-employment model

• Trainee experiences full responsibility of teaching in the sector.
• Trainee has the opportunity to earn while continuing training.

Challenges of teacher-in-training-and-paid-employment model

• Some trainees who gained L4 Stage 1 and 2 qualifications some time ago may not receive sufficient support in this model.
• Teacher trainers must be aware that procedures and expectations in some workplace settings may not provide the required models of good practice for the trainees.

Summary

In summary, Model 1 puts up to six trainees with their trainer and one group of learners. Models 2 and 3 allocate two to four trainees to one group of learners and a TP placement tutor. In Model 2, the trainees (as many as four) simultaneously teach small groups of the learners, whereas in Model 3 the two trainees take turns teaching the entire group. Model 4 is the traditional model with one trainee attached to one TP mentor and his/her class. Model 5 is often found at Level 4 Stage 3 training, with the teacher in paid employment during the training course . While in the first model the teacher trainer is always in the classroom and assesses the trainees, in the last four models described, the teacher trainer visits the group for the purpose of additional support and assessment. The TP mentor has no responsibility for summative assessment in these models.

The focus of this chapter has been to examine practical ways in which teaching practice placements can be improved. Phasing in individual teaching practice placements after group or paired placements and rigorously vetting placements make a valuable contribution to the overall improvement of teacher training in the Post-16 environment. Even if not all models can be provided on one course, giving trainees experience of more than one model during their training will greatly enhance their experience and give them a much-improved foundation for their teaching career.

Chapter 5
Observation of teaching practice: assessment and feedback

This chapter explores training for teacher trainers, with a particular focus on training for giving feedback to trainees on teaching practice. In **Equipping our Teachers** *the DfES Standards Unit advocates 'providing Continuing Professional Development (CPD) for teacher trainers, to ensure that they are fully up-to-date'. Although it is reassuring to see references to continuing professional development for teacher trainers, it cannot be assumed that they receive even initial training for their role. However, there is increasing recognition that teacher trainers should be carefully selected and trained before embarking on training and educating of others. A major component of this training should be in how to give both oral and written formal feedback on teaching practice.*

The DfES response to the November 2003 OFSTED report *The Initial Training of Further Education Teachers* stated that 'the entitlement of every trainee teacher should include an increase in the number of hours of teaching practice which are observed. A minimum is set but could be increased.' The recent DfES Standards Unit publication *Equipping our Teachers for the Future* sets an increased minimum standard:

Observation: an essential element of teacher training is the observation of the trainee's teaching and constructive feedback. There will be a minimum of eight observations during a full training course.... the teacher training team must decide when and by whom these observations take place, in order to support the trainee's learning most effectively.

From *Equipping our Teachers for the Future*, **DfES, 2004, paragraph 3.6**

We welcome the acknowledgment that more observations are needed. This chapter addresses issues on giving feedback to trainee teachers as a result of these TP observations.

Progress is being made in training trainers: there are now a number of specialist courses across the country, which train teacher trainers for their roles.

Talent London and LLU+ at London South Bank University have collaborated since 2001 and developed a Level 5 'Training the Literacy, ESOL and Numeracy Teacher Trainers' course. This programme is for experienced teachers of adult literacy, ESOL and numeracy wishing to train as specialist teacher trainers. The course comprises 12 days of training, and course participants need a practical placement on a Literacy, ESOL or Numeracy teacher training course. The programme includes the development of teacher training skills in general, plus subject specific work on the new Literacy, ESOL and Numeracy subject specifications.

The courses include the chance for participants to update their knowledge of teaching and learning theories whilst also working on the practical skills of supporting and assessing trainee teachers and designing and running teacher training sessions. The course is formally assessed through a series of assignments and practical observations. The 'Training the Teacher Trainers for Adult Literacy, ESOL and Numeracy' programme is validated by London South Bank University as a double unit (30 CATS points) at Level 5. *Talent London* approval as a teacher-trainer is also awarded to successful candidates

In addition to trainer training programmes offered to groups of new teacher-trainers, some accrediting bodies offer training programmes for individuals. Cambridge ESOL has a stringent selection procedure and training programme for all aspiring teacher trainers. Having been through the selection, the trainers in training are attached to an existing training programme, are assessed doing input sessions and giving feedback to trainees on their teaching practice. They are also required to complete a portfolio of assignments, which is externally assessed. This programme ensures that trainee trainers are fully appraised before they become accredited teacher trainers.

A substantial objective of any 'training the teacher training' course or approval programme should be to prepare teacher trainers to give oral and written feedback to their trainees after teaching practice. This will include giving formative and summative assessment. The responsibility for giving summative feedback to trainee teachers and assessing their teaching practice should rest solely with the teacher trainers of the course. They have a thorough knowledge of the standards set by the awarding body and the course requirements. In addition, because they are teaching the trainees, they know exactly what it is realistic to expect of them, depending on the stage of the course.

Giving effective, supportive feedback to developing teachers requires considerable skill. In order to become proficient in giving feedback, they themselves will need training. The training should cover assessing teaching practice against set criteria as well as how to convey the feedback. In addition, this training should enable trainers to distinguish between feedback to trainee teachers and other types of feedback, for example, that given to qualified teachers during an appraisal. Without an opportunity to reflect on their role, inexperienced trainers may look to appraisals based on LLUK standards as a model for TP observations. 'The standards developed by LLUK are a description of the role of an experienced teacher, not a definition of the outcomes of initial training.' (*Equipping our Teachers for the Future*, DfES, 2004)

Some training, in the form of standardisation meetings, is provided by the awarding bodies for their teacher trainers. These cover not only assignment marking but also feedback on teaching practice. Teacher trainers may watch a video of teaching, assess it against the criteria and then discuss the points which should be raised with that trainee. The scope of these standardisation meetings may cover strengths and areas for improvement for the trainee but will normally not encompass how to give feedback. The assumption is that the teacher trainer will already possess those skills. However, those new to teacher training will need to acquire them. It is another item on the growing agenda of ways to improve initial teacher training.

Through such courses or sessions organised by awarding bodies, many teacher-trainers may therefore have been observed themselves while giving oral formal feedback to trainees after the trainees have taught a group of learners. Through case studies, role-plays and identifying good practice in giving feedback, teacher-trainers develop invaluable expertise in how to give oral feedback.

Teacher trainers develop and hone their skills by participating in activities with other trainers and through collective reflection on their work. This is one of the key justifications for supporting trainer networks. Trainers support and give one another constructive criticism, for example, while role-playing giving feedback. Once in the training position within their institutions, new trainers may have little support and can feel isolated. Trainer training courses can therefore provide peer support and guidance from more experienced teacher trainers at a crucial stage.

As mentioned previously, new or would-be trainers on a trainer training course should be able to practise assessing teaching practice against set criteria. The criteria may come from the accrediting body or, at the early stages of training, there may be scope for the trainers to develop subject-specific criteria. A set of criteria from the Cambridge ESOL Certificate in Further Education Teaching Level 4 Stage 3 with the Certificate for ESOL Subject Specialists is shown overleaf.

**Certificate in Further Education Teaching Stage 3
with the Certificate for ESOL Subject Specialists**

Excerpted from Candidate Record Booklet

Candidates can:

a **plan lessons which:**
  i *have clearly expressed outcomes derived from the learning programme*
  ii *relate to learner needs and learning styles*
  iii *serve as a procedural guide for the lesson and a record of it*
  iv *Include developmental aims for the teacher*

b **teach effectively by:**
  i *creating a positive, safe, and purposeful learning environment which is inclusive of all learners*
  ii *managing the learning process to achieve stated learning outcomes, while making appropriate modifications in response to the classroom dynamic*
  iii *using a range of teaching and learning techniques*
  iv *setting tasks and activities - whole class, group, and individual learning, and creating opportunities for experiential learning outside the classroom*
  v *using resources to support learning*
  vi *communicating effectively with learners*
  vii *monitoring learning and providing feedback*
  viii *ensuring own practice promotes equality of opportunity and addresses the needs of all learners*
  ix *reviewing the learning process with learners*
  x *assessing the learners' achievement in relation to lesson objectives and the overall learning programme and using the information to plan future learning*
  xi *critically evaluating their teaching in the FE context based on self-evaluations and reflections and feedback on their teaching from peers and superiors and from their learners*

c **demonstrate competent subject-specific teaching skills by**
  i *accurately analysing language for teaching purposes, using correct terminology relating to grammar, lexis and phonology and in the analysis of extended spoken and written discourse*
  ii *presenting language in contexts which are relevant and interesting to learners*
  iii *Focusing on a wider range of language items in the classroom including, where appropriate, a discourse analysis perspective*
  iv *using a wide range of approaches, methods, strategies and techniques appropriately to develop learners' language awareness and use*

> *v* developing learners' awareness of all four language skills and sub-skills and the relationship between them
>
> *vi* selecting and using culturally appropriate materials taking account of learner background, interests and level
>
> *vii* using a wide range of approaches, methods, strategies and techniques appropriately to develop learners' receptive and productive skills
>
> *viii* highlighting for learners the value of written and spoken texts as sources of language and culture
>
> **d show an appropriate knowledge and use of English by:**
>
> *i* using English effectively when communicating with speakers of other languages
>
> *ii* adjusting own use of English as appropriate to the level of understanding of the interlocutor
>
> *iii* using a range of strategies to make meaning clear, when presenting and communicating new information
>
> *iv* providing appropriate models and examples of language use, to assist the language development of the learners
>
> *v* assisting others to communicate and express themselves accurately, through the use of feedback, correction, reformulation
>
> *vi* using a range of strategies, including checking questions to confirm understanding

With any set of criteria, there is the risk of feedback becoming a series of tickboxes. One way of avoiding this is for the lesson-planning pro-forma used by trainees to have a column for the trainer's comments. The trainer will have a copy of the criteria as well as a copy of the trainee's lesson plan during the teaching practice observation. As the trainer watches the lesson, s/he can make observations as to the strengths or weaknesses of that particular part of the lesson. A copy of this annotated lesson plan will be given to the trainee as part of the formal feedback. This is successful as trainees appreciate receiving detailed feedback on each stage of the lesson, rather than reading general comments, which might apply to any part of the lesson. It allows them to feel confident about those elements which went well and focus on specific areas of development.

Teacher training teams need to consider a range of pro-formas which balance the needs of trainees against those of the trainers. Although it may be convenient for the teacher trainer to simply indicate whether or not the criteria have been met, from the trainee's point of view, comments about each stage of the lesson enable them to learn more from the feedback

At the end of the written feedback, there should be sufficient space for a summary of the trainer's comments. Trainees regard this section of written feedback as the essence of their evaluation. Some guidelines devised on the **talent London**/LLU+ Training the Teacher Trainers 2003–4 course appear below.

Guidelines for TP feedback summaries

1   *A good summary gives a sense of the whole lesson or that part of it which was observed.*
2   *Set out action points as numbered bullet points and not 'a body of text'.*
3   *Summarise strengths first.*
4   *Weaknesses/points to work on should be selected and phrased as targets which should be prioritised.*
5   *The tone should be positive and supportive overall.*
6   *Avoid subjective, overly personal comments and angry tones.*
7   *Avoid comments like, 'You shouldn't...', 'Why didn't you...?', 'Why did you...?' and, 'You must...' Where possible/appropriate, say how changes could be made, rather than just stating that they should be made; for example, 'How about x...?', 'Try doing y...', or 'Remember to ...'.*
8   *Mention how the learners experienced the lesson.*
9   *If the lesson is particularly weak, the summary must state that the lesson was below the standard required.*
10   *The feedback summary should not be too wordy.*
11   *The feedback should be appropriate to the stage of the course and to the stage of the trainee's development.*
12   *Feedback should relate to the established criteria of the accrediting body.*
13   *Feedback should be neat, legible and have no crossings out.*
14   *General points should be supported by clear examples.*
15   *Criticisms should be in the form of targets set.*
16   *Feedback should always be re-read to see if it provides the appropriate 'audit trail'.*
17   *Be very clear about what the trainee has to do to meet the standards.*

talent London and LLU+ at LSBU

Considerable skill is required on the part of the trainer to achieve effective summaries. One activity used on trainer training courses is to provide groups with a range of examples of TP feedback summaries. Each summary is discussed and evaluated against the above guidelines. The trainee trainers then re-draft the feedback summaries.

To sum up:

- Teacher trainers should be entitled to a thorough and accredited training programme in order to fulfil their role. This training should provide them with the opportunity to become skilful in giving oral as well as written feedback to their trainees, feedback which should be pitched at the appropriate level and stage of the training.
- TP mentors should also receive training in carrying out observations and how to give developmental feedback to trainees.
- Trainee teachers should be observed a minimum of eight times per year and should receive developmental as well as summative observations.
- Formal assessment of teaching practice should be against set criteria suitable for the stage of the teacher training course.
- In future, all teacher trainers should be trained in the role of formal assessor before being employed.
- All provider organisations should aim to have well-trained trainers among their staff teams: this usually produces raised standards among teachers in general, by encouraging all members of staff to adopt best practice, and by being role models for professional and career development.
- Realistic funding for these measures should be made available.

Chapter 6
Training for teaching practice mentors

This chapter presents a range of approaches and materials for the training of teaching practice mentors, based on experiences in the London region and the three RETRO regions. These are not comprehensive and are offered as ideas to be built on and developed rather than as best practice.

The type of training which TP mentors are able or required to attend depends, of course, on what is expected of them in their role. Assuming they are not formally assessing the trainees, the TP mentors should have at least three to six hours of training. The one-day course in the RETRO Eastern region includes:

• the role of the mentor
• the qualities and skills of a mentor
• initial support for mentees
• record-keeping
• information feedback on classroom observations
• action planning

During the day, the participants produce a course plan, a sample mentoring record form, an observation checklist and a roles/responsibilities/dispositions list.

As most TP mentors will give oral, developmental feedback, however, they should be clear on the headings they use for this feedback.

Below is a set of guidelines for a typical placement tutor observation :

Key observation criteria

Did the tutor:
- *Arrive on time, prepare properly and set up the room?*
- *Write a lesson plan with clear objectives?*
- *Elicit learners' relevant experience and knowledge as a starting point for teaching and learning?*
- *Take account of the different learning needs and styles in the group?*
- *Communicate well with learners?*
- *Establish a good rapport?*
- *Use relevant methods and teach at the right pace ?*
- *Make or select materials with relevant content and at the right level?*
- *Manage both group and individual learning?*
- *Give learners accurate and constructive feedback on progress?*
- *Encourage students to self assess and to give feedback on their learning?*
- *Complete appropriate records?*

City Lit TP Mentor Training

Here is another version from RETRO Eastern region which provides the TP mentor with a list of prompts.

Classroom observation prompts

The working environment
- *Was the teacher in the classroom to meet the students?*
- *Was there a set procedure for students entering and leaving the classroom?*
- *How did the teacher get students started on the task?*
- *Were the materials to be used in the lesson organised, clearly labelled and ready to use?*
- *What pattern(s) of classroom organisation did you observe: individual/ group/class teaching?*
- *If parents or ancillary staff were involved, how did it work?*

The physical environment
- *How was the classroom set out?*
- *Did the classroom present a pleasant learning environment?*
- *Did the layout of the classroom help or hinder students?*
- *How far did the displays of work connect to the planning and delivery of the curriculum?*
- *Did the noise level hinder any parties from working?*

Activity related factors – students
To what extent did the students:
- *Understand the objectives of the lesson?*
- *Understand the instructions given?*
- *Display interest and enthusiasm for the task(s)?*
- *Display a friendly, confident and relaxed attitude towards the teacher?*
- *Cope with the activities set?*
- *Reach an acceptable level of attainment?*
- *Know the procedures and routines of the classroom?*
- *Behave appropriately?*
- *Work co-operatively with the teacher and other students?*
- *Refer to other students for help?*
- *Move from one activity to another by responding to instructions?*

Activity related factors – the teacher
To what extent did the teacher:
- *Display a firm but friendly and relaxed attitude towards the students?*
- *Secure and retain the attention of the students?*
- *Time the lesson or individual activities appropriately?*
- *Pace the lesson appropriately?*

- *Provide for progressive learning?*
- *Manage the differences in students' abilities?*
- *Use praise and other forms of encouragement or rewards?*
- *Provide opportunities for students to take responsibility for their own learning?*
- *Move around the classroom to assist individuals or groups?*
- *Move around the classroom to maintain discipline?*
- *Anticipate and avoid inappropriate behaviour?*
- *Deal with minor interruptions?*
- *Allow students to comment on their own work or learning?*
- *Incorporate multi-cultural issues into the lesson?*
- *Demonstrate a variety of teaching materials?*
- *Provide clear instructions?*
- *Use students' responses to enhance learning?*
- *Use the activities to assess the students' progress?*
- *Use it as an integral part of teaching and learning?*

Communication factors
To what extent did the teacher:
- *Use vocabulary understood by the students?*
- *Allow for the participation of all students?*
- *Use clarifying questions?*
- *Use leading questions?*
- *Use questions to assess students' understanding and progress?*
- *Ask questions which encouraged imaginative responses?*
- *Prompt students when appropriate?*
- *Use students' responses to encourage further discussions?*
- *Reward questions and answers?*
- *Use a clear, audible and interesting voice?*
- *Provide clear instructions and expectations?*

RETRO Eastern Region TP Mentor training

These are useful prompts to help a TP mentor provide developmental feedback. Below are brief descriptions of some other activities which can be used in the training of TP mentors.

1. Lessons on video
The group watch a numeracy, literacy or ESOL lesson on video with the TP mentors. They then discuss the strengths of the lesson and consider appropriate feedback for different stages of the trainee teacher's placement, i.e. Is this the first lesson with the learners? What should be highlighted in informal feedback? If it is the 10th lesson, what oral feedback would be appropriate?

2. Role plays

Trainers write role cards with a brief scenario and a mood for both the trainee teacher and the placement tutor. Some centres also have an observer in the role-play to contribute to comments at the end. The scenarios are then acted out in pairs or threes and discussed. One key objective of this activity is to raise awareness of the importance of emphasising the positive and praising the trainees. Inexperienced mentors, and even some new trainers, may err on the side of spotting areas for improvement, rather than stating strengths.

3. Slips to sort

Groups are given sets of slips with responsibilities on them – groups decide which are responsibilities for TP placement tutors and which are responsibilities for the teacher training course team. Groups compare their conclusions.

4. Case studies

Groups are given some realistic case studies and points for discussion. For example:

Case study for teaching practice placement tutor training

Shana

Shana is much loved by the students in your group. She is warm and helpful. However, she consistently comes late and leaves early. She has missed several sessions and you are worried she will not complete her 20 hours of teaching practice. Her difficulty seems to be with childcare and travel.

She was supposed to lead part of the session this week, but she forgot and has come unprepared. You had to do it instead.

1. *What strengths and areas for development would you want to feed back to Shana?*
2. *What evidence would you use to back up your points?*
3. *Complete your feedback planner for the difficult part.*

Case study from talent London

---

5. Sharing ideas

The group is set the task of deciding what makes a good numeracy/literacy/ESOL class. This is a good way for the group to agree on what standards they think trainees should aim for.

6. Activity to raise awareness of the trainee teacher's point of view

This activity works well at the beginning of the training session with new teaching practice placement tutors. This is how it works.

Preparation

Before the training session with TP placement tutors, the trainers should do a bit of preparation with a group of trainee teachers facing their first teaching practice placements. Elicit from them the concerns and questions they have about starting their placements.
Some examples:

• How will I be treated by the students? Will they know I've never taught before?
• What will the other staff think of me – will they think I'm a nuisance?
• Will there be resistance and resentment of me – from the students – as I'm not their normal teacher?
• Will I have to go straight into a group I don't know?
• Can I watch the class teacher first?
• How will I know what to teach?
• What if there's an argument between students in the class?
• What shall I do if I have discipline problems?
• What can I do if I can't answer the students' questions?
• What if I run out of material before the end of my lesson?
• What if I get 'stage fright' and can't 'go on'?

Take the list to the teaching practice placement training session.

Task in small groups or pairs

• Ask the trainee placement tutors to work in small groups or pairs and to have a look at the list of concerns and questions new trainee teachers have about their first teaching practice placement.

• Discuss how the placement tutor could help.

Whole-group feedback

• As a whole group: pull out some of the most important suggestions – onto a flip chart, OHT, interactive whiteboard.

Or:

• Cross-group – pass on suggestions to another group.
• Do they agree or have anything to add? Add to the list of suggestions.

Key points

• This gives us the beginning of the 'role description' of a teaching practice placement tutor;
• and shows how the experience, expertise and confidence that teachers have is essential to the support and nurture of new teachers.

Extension

The list could be matched against a more formal job/role description for a teaching practice placement tutor:
• Does it match?
• What additional things are there?
• This takes the session into the next stage: looking at the requirements of a teacher training course, and those of the awarding body.

This chapter has covered a range of practical issues surrounding the definition of the role of the TP mentor and given examples from various training programmes to help the TP mentors fulfil their role. It cannot be emphasised enough that the success of teaching practice often depends on the TP mentor. It follows, therefore, that the role must carry high status within institutions and ideally payment and remission. It should be a role that excellent practitioners aspire to and for which they are selected. Once selected, these would-be TP mentors deserve high-quality training and support from the teacher training team. They will then become confident and skilled in their role and will be in a better position to help trainees to become confident and skilled themselves. Achieving this will require a cultural shift within many institutions, but the benefits of embedding successful TP mentoring are enormous, creating a virtuous circle of expertise and capacity-building within the institution.

In the early 1990s, Kent Adult Education Service developed an excellent mentoring programme. Experienced adult education tutors were invited to train as mentors to new tutors. The training course was accredited by the School of Continuing Education at the University of Kent at Canterbury. The scheme was a huge success and ran for about five years. Tutors who benefited from having 'a mentor' still refer back to how valuable the experience was for them. Mentors also found the work very rewarding. Unfortunately, mentoring was discontinued because it was considered too expensive.

Sue Huston, ex-mentor, Kent Adult Education Service

Chapter 7
Developing new teaching practice and mentoring placements

This chapter outlines the importance of continuing to develop new teaching practice placement opportunities, and of placements in a wider range of settings, so that newly-qualified teachers have had experience of teaching in settings other than colleges. Examples are given of the ways in which some regional partnerships have addressed this issue.

In order to improve the quality of teacher training for LLN teachers, we need to go beyond reforms called for in Chapter 4 – phasing in apprentice-style teaching practice – and those outlined in Chapters 5 and 6 – improving the quality of teaching practice observation and feedback, and developing specific training for mentors. In addition, it is essential to broaden the **range** of placement settings experienced by trainee teachers.

At present, when a teacher qualifies, whatever the route they have followed, they are formally accredited to teach in any setting. LLN teachers work in family centres, in community classes, in discrete programmes within further education colleges, on LLN programmes embedded in a vast range of vocational training courses, in prisons, in work-based learning situations, in private and public sector businesses, and with learners as young as 14 or 15 years old. The vast majority of newly qualified teachers, however, will have received all their teaching practice experience in one setting only, and that setting will, in most cases, be a college of further education. The trainees would benefit from a system which reflected the variety of employment prospects, and so would the learners.

In most areas, at present, it is seen as the responsibility of individual training providers to organise teaching practice placements for their trainee teachers. Some of these pass on this responsibility to the trainees, who are thus often required to find their own placements. This is hit and miss at best, and even if trainees can find placements they may well find themselves in situations where they receive little support and are forced into some poor practice. Although some colleges undertake to find placements for their trainees and to screen these placements, lack of funding means this is far from the norm. A much more systematic approach is needed to underpin this essential element of teacher training is, based on sharing resources through partnership.

Teaching practice placements should, ideally, be developed, allocated, co-ordinated and quality-assured at a regional level. Experience from the RETRO regions and from **talent London** strongly suggests that co-ordination of effort through a regional partnership of stakeholders is the most effective way to make the best use of existing resources, and develop new capacity; the stock of high-quality placements for teaching practice available to initial teacher trainees is just one example. Such a regional partnership should in the first place establish the level of need, within a strategic projection of the volume of training courses required in the region to support the national *Skills for Life* strategy. This survey should also note the location of each available placement, so that employers from a range of different sectors (including Job Centre Plus, prisons, public- and private-sector businesses) can then be approached in order to involve them in providing new placements for those in the later stages of their training. This will enrich the experience for trainees as well as increasing the number of newly qualified teachers who apply for employment outside colleges. The RETRO project provides an effective model for a programme of placements which is co-ordinated at regional level.

In the RETRO project in the North East Region, a small team of 'teacher-educators' has been appointed jointly between the Universities of Northumbria, Sunderland, and Teesside. Their key tasks are:

- to work alongside university staff to identify, select, arrange and manage student teacher placements;
- to quality assure teacher training placements and to ensure regional consistency of practice;
- to monitor and evaluate teacher training placements and to make recommendations for improvements; and
- to provide training and mentor support to the teaching practice mentors themselves.

As part of finding and developing new teaching practice placements they work to support improvements in these locations (often in community-based or workplace settings) to satisfy an agreed set of quality criteria. This model is being evaluated as part of the RETRO project, but as a result of this initiative not only have sufficient placements been identified for all RETRO trainees, in many cases it has been possible to give trainees experience of teaching practice in more than one setting, thus directly addressing one of the main weaknesses identified in the OFSTED review. The role of the teacher educator in terms of placement support is vital to the trainees. The teacher educator is directly involved both in the support and training of the mentors to enable them to facilitate their role successfully with workplace trainees. The teacher educator provides a back up to trainees when issues around placement arise and the trainees feel supported knowing that the teacher educator is just a phone call away. The teacher educator provides the vital link between the placement experience and the university experience for the trainees.

Sharon Powell, University of Teesside

In the early stages of their training, trainees themselves can be set a mini-research task of surveying different types of employment. As a group, they can put together a list of possible employers in the area. They can then interview some of them and report back or the employers could be asked to come in to meet the trainees and describe the work.

In other regions, small amounts of project funding or capacity-building funding have been used to 'incentivise' providers to agree to offer teaching-practice placements. These resources have in some cases been paid directly to teaching-practice mentors (typically a notional contract for half an hour per week for each trainee), and in other cases to providers to enable remission from teaching to be extended to teaching-practice mentors and to cover other organisational overheads. This kind of incentive approach has worked well, and costs relatively little, though of course these initiatives depend once again on short-term project funding and create difficulties at the end of such funding cycles, especially if the funding cannot be continued.

The development of new teaching practice placements, especially in under-represented sectors, is likely to be a critical element of developing expanded LLN teacher training opportunities in most regions. Tackling this can be tied into regional marketing and widening-participation strategies, aimed, for example, at workplaces and at community organisations, especially those in which LLN may be a central part of capacity-building, but for whom the provision of learning is not their primary focus. As well as sites for the development of new LLN programmes, these 'non-educational' organisations should be developed as locations for new teaching-practice placements as well. This in turn should encourage a wider range of people to consider training as LLN teachers, thus producing a virtuous circle of capacity-building which can have spin-offs in terms of economic and cultural regeneration, in workforce development, and in improved social cohesion, far beyond the narrow focus of *Skills for Life* targets. This virtuous circle is unlikely to be established without a stable regional strategic partnership of all key stakeholders based on trust and a common understanding of the benefits of working in this way. With this, the supply of high-quality and diversely-situated teaching practice placements is likely to be well-developed.

Chapter 8
Quality assurance for teaching practice and mentoring

This chapter suggests areas of planning and provision of teaching practice and mentoring that need to be covered by quality assurance standards and procedures, and gives examples of documentation from two RETRO regions.

Quality assurance is important for two reasons: firstly, the existing institutional quality standards are probably generic, applying to all programmes delivered by that institution, and based on a norm of class-based provision. If this is so, then many aspects of teaching practice and mentoring are unlikely to be covered.

The second reason that this is a critical issue is that in many cases the programmes are being delivered as a partnership between two or more organisations, each of which probably has its own statement of quality standards and procedures, which may or not be mutually compatible. The process of developing approaches to quality assurance between two or more organisations is itself a rich process of professional development, and the achievement of agreed standards and procedures across organisations and partnerships is a critical factor in achieving consistency of practice.

Over time we want to create a network of Centres of Excellence in Teacher Training (CETT). We anticipate that these CETTs will provide:

1. *strong effective leadership and management;*
2. *a track record of success in workforce development;*
3. *good practice and high standards;*
4. *expertise across a range of learning contexts;*
5. *taking a lead in active local partnerships.*

Given that we are aiming for a step-change in the quality of training for teachers across the whole of the learning and skills sector, the emphasis upon local partnerships is vital. It will enable trainee teachers whose own employer may not meet CETT criteria to have the opportunity to learn with others working in different organisations, in the same subject or occupational area, as a key aspect of their initial development

Adapted from *Equipping our Teachers for the Future*, DfES, 2004

What follows is a suggested checklist of different aspects of teaching practice and mentoring which each need an explicit set of quality standards and procedures. This is accompanied by two samples of quality standards for different aspects of the work that have been developed and operated by partnerships within the RETRO project.

1. Teaching practice

• Minimum quality standards for organisations providing teaching practice placements.
• Procedures for monitoring the quality of teaching practice placements.
• Procedures for formal observations, feedback and assessment of teaching practice.
• Quality standards for staff carrying out formal observations of teaching practice.
• Minimum standards for volume and range of teaching practice opportunities for each trainee.
• Standards for the professional support of mentors supporting teaching practice.
• Procedures for applying checks against the criminal records disclosure register in relation to trainees working in placements with vulnerable learners.
• Personal and public liability insurance covering trainees on teaching practice.

2. Mentoring

• Selection criteria for mentors.
• Quality standards for mentoring, formative assessment and feedback of trainees.
• A professional code of practice for mentors.

The RETRO project in the North East Region

Teaching-practice placement, checklist of Quality Criteria

- *To be an employer of experienced and qualified LLN teachers working to the Skills for Life Agenda*
- *To actively use the Adult Core Curriculum, be able to offer a range of non-accredited and accredited courses including National Tests, have experience of initial and diagnostic learner assessment, and to make use of individual learning plans and records of progress reviews.*
- *To be able to provide a range of teaching and learning opportunities with learners from pre-entry to level 2*
- *To hold public and personal liability insurance that will cover student teachers when in placement.*
- *The ability to provide student teachers with a minimum of _____ hours teaching practice per week split between group (groups of six or more) and one-to-one teaching.*
- *To be able to offer all teaching between _____ and _____ .*
- *To provide a named mentor to support, encourage, review progress of and informally monitor the progress of each student teacher.*
- *To agree to participate in mentoring training, provided by the appropriate university.*
- *To be able to provide student teacher access to workspace and an Internet-linked computer.*
- *To nominate a named link to work with the project team, teacher-educator consultants and academic staff to monitor qualitatively the student teacher and the placement process. This will involve some data recording and report production.*

A Professional Code of Practice for Mentors

- *The mentoring relationship is a professional partnership and should be treated as such. A professional, well organised mentor, who can ascertain the needs of the mentee and respond accordingly, can make the difference between failure and success for the mentee. Furthermore, the mentoring meeting is committed time, and part of the mentee's training entitlement.*
- *A mentor should arrange regular meetings with their mentee, in accordance with organisational policies.*
- *Mentoring meetings should be arranged for a designated time and place.*
- *If unavoidable circumstances mean that the mentoring meeting cannot go ahead at the usual time, it should be rescheduled for the next available opportunity.*
- *A mentor should arrive for mentoring meetings punctually.*
- *A mentor should arrive prepared for the agreed meeting.*
- *Mentors should give mentees their undivided attention: carrying out other tasks whilst discussing things with the mentee or taking phone calls during mentoring time should be avoided.*
- *Mentoring meetings should have a definite focus.*
- *The mentor and mentee should set the mentoring agenda together. A mentor should respond to the developmental needs of the mentee and should not impose their own issues or concerns on the mentoring time.*
- *A mentor should adhere to organisational policies regarding confidentiality.*
- *A mentor should not pay lip-service to paperwork which records the mentoring time but should record meetings in a way which allows the mentee to develop by using it for future reference and reflection.*
- *A mentor should never exploit the mentoring relationship and should guard against the exploitation of the mentee by other parties.*
- *A mentor must realise their own limitations and request the help of others from within their organisation in order to meet the developmental needs of the mentee.*
- *A mentor has a duty of care towards the mentee and should help the mentee deal with any emotional responses triggered by the training process.*
- *A mentor should handle any problems concerning the mentoring process in a professional manner and in accordance with the quality assurance procedures within their organisation.*

Association of Colleges in the Eastern Region, Teacher Training Unit
Mentoring Handbook, **at page 16**
http://www.acer.ac.uk/newtrainingthetrainers/training_material.html

Appendix 1

Useful publications

The initial training of further education teachers, a survey, OFSTED, 2003 available at www.ofsted.gov.uk/publications/index.cfm?fuseaction=pubs.summary&id= 3425 [accessed 21 July 2005].

Equipping our teachers for the future: reforming initial teacher training for the learning and skills sector, DfES 2004, available at http://www.successforall.gov.uk/downloads/equippingourteachersforthefut ure-115-161.pdf [accessed 21 July 2005].

Addressing language, literacy and numeracy needs in education and training: defining the minimum core of teachers' knowledge, understanding and personal skill, a guide for teacher education programmes, LLUK 2004, available at http://www.lifelonglearninguk.org/documents/svukdocs/minimum_core_ guide_for_itt_programmes.pdf [accessed 21 July 2005].

'The role of intuition in mentoring and supporting beginning teachers', Elisabeth Lazarus, in *The Intuitive Practitioner*, eds T Atkinson and G Claxton, Open University Press, 2003.

Funding guidance for further education in 2004/05, LSC briefing paper on how learning aims are allocated listed funding rates, May 2004, available at www.lsc.gov.uk/National/Documents/SubjectListing/FundingLearning /FurtherEducation/Funding_Guidance04_05.htm [accessed 21 July 2005].

*The **Skills for Life** survey: a national needs and impact survey of literacy, numeracy and ICT skills*, Research Report 490, DfES 2003, available at www.dfes.gov.uk/research/data/uploadfiles/RR490.pdf [accessed 21 July 2005].

Literacy, numeracy and English for speakers of other languages: a survey of current practice in Post 16 and Adult provision, OFSTED, September 2003, available at www.ofsted.gov.uk/publications/ [accessed 21 July 2005].

Mentoring towards excellence, LSC, AoC and LLUK 2001, available from the LSC, ref number P/0005/01.

Wolverhampton University on-line mentoring manual: this project is developing high-quality e-learning resources to support the planning and delivery of mentoring training. This resource is being supplemented with key units on observation of teachers and coaching skills in each *Skills for Life* subject. For more information, contact Karl Royle on k.royle@wlv.ac.uk

'The impact of quality assurance on mentor training in initial teacher education partnerships: a UK perspective', Bernadette Youens and Mary Bailey, University of Nottingham, *Canadian Journal of Educational Administration and Policy*, Issue 32, July 2004.

Reflective teaching in further and adult education, Yvonne Hillier, Continuum 2002.

Educating the reflective practitioner, Donald A Schön, Jossey Bass, 1987.

Developing professional knowledge and competence, Michael Eraut, Falmer Press, 1999.

Mentoring handbook, East of England *Skills for Life* Regional Training Project, available at www.acer.ac.uk/newtrainingthetrainers/training_material.html [accessed 21 July 2005].

References

'Providing support for student interdependence through scaffolded instruction'. Martha Larkin, *Teaching Exceptional Children*, Volume 34, pages 30–34, 2001.

The ontogenesis of speech acts', J.S. Bruner, *Journal of Child Language*, Volume 2, pages 1–40, 1975.

'The use of scaffolds for teaching higher level cognitive strategies', B. Rosenshine and C. Meister, *Educational Leadership*, Volume 49, Issue 7, pages 26–33, 1992.

Appendix 2

Useful contacts and websites

DfES	www.dfes.gov.uk/readwriteplus/
LLU+	www.lsbu.ac.uk/lluplus/
LLUK (formerly FENTO)	www.lifelonglearninguk.org/
LSC	www.lsc.gov.uk
LSDA	www.lsda.org.uk
NIACE	www.niace.org.uk
NRDC	www.nrdc.org.uk/
OFSTED	www.ofsted.gov.uk/
RETRO	www.niace.org.uk/projects/RETRO/
Skills for Life	www.dfes.gov.uk/readwriteplus/
Skills for Life Quality Initiative	http://www.sflqi.org.uk
Success for All	www.successforall.gov.uk/
talent London	www.talent.ac.uk

Appendix 3

Glossary

ABSSU (now SFLSU)	The *Skills for Life* Strategy Unit, based within the DfES
CETT	Centres of Excellence in Teacher Training
DfES	Department for Education and Skills
HEI	Higher Education Institution, ie a university
LLN	Literacy, language and numeracy
LLU+	The London Language and Literacy Unit at London South Bank University
LLUK	Lifelong Learning UK (formerly FENTO)
LSC	The Learning and Skills Council
LSDA	The Learning and Skills Development Agency
NIACE	The National Institute of Adult Continuing Education
NQF	The National Qualifications Framework for England, Wales and Northern Ireland sets out the levels at which all formal qualifications can be recognised.
NRDC	National Research and Development Centre for adult literacy and numeracy
OFSTED	The Office for Standards in Education
QCA	The Qualifications and Curriculum Authority
RETRO	A regional teacher training development project funded by ABSSU/SfLSU between September 03 and March 05
Skills for Life	The national strategy for improving adult literacy, language and numeracy, directed by the *Skills for Life* Strategy Unit within the DfES
SfLQI	The *Skills for Life* Quality Initiative, supporting continuous professional development for LLN teachers.
Success for All	The DfES programme to improve quality across the learning and skills sector
talent London	The literacy, ESOL and numeracy teacher training co-ordination project for London